D1565370

# CYNTHIA ANN PARKER

*Indian Captive*

Stories

For Young

Americans

# CYNTHIA ANN PARKER,

## INDIAN CAPTIVE

by

## Catherine Troxell Gonzalez

*Stories For Young*

*Americans Series*

Drawings By Virginia Scott Gholson

EAKIN PRESS      ★      AUSTIN, TEXAS

# TABLE OF CONTENTS

# 1. Life As A Young Comanche Girl

Small puffs of dust rose from the old buffalo trail as the Comanche Indian tribe wound down the canyon wall. The men rode their fast ponies at the head of the column, followed by the wives and children at a much slower pace. Occasionally, one of the boys would urge his pony out to the side in a gallop as he chased a rabbit or prairie dog. There was much laughter and shouting among the younger children. Everyone enjoyed the excitement of moving to a new camp. The previous day had been a hard one for the men of the tribe. The raid at Fort Parker had taken much of their energy away from them.

After the first night and day of horror, it seemed to the child, Cynthia Ann, who had been taken in at the raid, that they rode for days and days. At night they rested. Cynthia Ann and John, her brother, were tied with rawhide. In a few weeks, however, John was given to another tribe. Babies and young white children were very much desired by the Indians, who lost many of their own to illness.

It was to be some time before Cynthia Ann was treated with anything like kindness. She remained for the most part in a state of shock. She just sat on the ground, neither talking nor playing. This life seemed very strange to her. For a long time her captors treated her badly. She was cuffed and slapped for no reason. She learned to cry very quietly so that they would not notice her. The days and nights seemed very long. Sometimes she thought about her home. But she soon learned that such thoughts just made her sad.

Slowly, the past became dim in her mind, and she seldom thought of her mother and her father.

The tribe moved very often. Food and water were always hard to find. Many days Cynthia Ann went hungry. The old woman with whom she lived sometimes threw her a piece of raw meat. At first it went uneaten. She could not look at the raw, hot meat. She dug for roots and sometimes she was allowed to hunt for berries. The old woman showed Cynthia Ann where to find berries and which roots to dig.

The meals were very different from those in Cynthia Ann's home. The Comanches always ate with their fingers. Often, the food was not cooked. When a buffalo was butchered, they ate the liver and the heart raw. They did not waste any part of the buffalo. The hide was tanned for use as robes, tepees, or bedding. The hoofs and horns were made into weapons. The women and children ate after the men were through with the food. Cynthia Ann sometimes was lucky to get her share before it was thrown to the dogs.

Old Woman was the first person to show kindness toward the lonely little girl. She often helped Cynthia Ann with the work that was assigned to her. The other Indians were slower to accept the girl. They finally became less cruel when they talked to her. The younger children tried to talk to her and to play with her. They taught her some of their games. They quit playing tricks on her. Life became a little easier for Cynthia Ann.

It was strange to sleep on the grass under the stars. At night she was still tied to a stake, but now they tried to give her a spot with soft grass. Months passed before her captors allowed her to sleep without the rawhide straps.

Often the tribe camped beside a small stream. Cynthia Ann was allowed to bathe in the water. She felt good on those days. The women laughed at her when she washed her face. They didn't wash theirs. Slowly, Cynthia Ann was becoming used to their ways. She thought that perhaps someday she wouldn't wash her face.

Cynthia Ann still thought of her papa and her mama. It seemed so far away. Her cool, soft bed at home became only a dim memory. Sometimes sleeping under the stars was pleasant. The grass was soft and cool. In the winter the Indians huddled warmly under a buffalo robe.

Old Woman taught her many new ways. As Cynthia Ann grew older, she saw the difference in her coloring and that of the reddish brown Indian skin. She began to dye her skin and hair with clay and berry juice. She rubbed the red clay on her face to make it darker. Old Woman sometimes allowed her to sleep inside the tepee.

Summers were more pleasant than winters. The tribe went north to follow the buffalo herds. They worked hard tanning the skins for use in the winters. Cynthia Ann learned to scrape and chew the hide to make it soft and pretty. The tribe kept very few belongings, but the buffalo hides were a useful item. They packed them on dog travois or sleds to move their belongings from one camp to another.

The buffalo herds were the center of Indian life. Their tepees were made of hides draped over tall poles. In moving, they used the poles to make a travois for the dogs to pull. The tribe's clothing and

bedding were carried in that way. Although they ate other food, the Indians needed the buffalo for their very lives.

In the summer time there was plenty to eat, but during the long, cold winters, the tribe usually moved south. The weather was not so bad in the hills of south Texas. There was not so much food, but they escaped some of the snow and ice. They could kill antelope, deer, even rabbits and squirrels.

One day when Cynthia Ann had been with the Comanches for about four years, Old Woman called to her to follow. Quiet, as she usually was, Cynthia Ann walked behind Old Woman to the place where the elders were talking with some white men. Because they stared at her, Cynthia Ann hid behind Old Woman. She was afraid of these men with white skins. Old Woman had told her never to talk with anyone except the People, as the Comanches called themselves.

Besides that, their voices sounded harsh and strange. The sounds they made were no longer real to the young girl. Her mind had blotted out all memory of a language that had not been heard for so many months.

One of the men motioned for her to come toward him. She shook her head, but the chief, who had been talking with the men, told her to come forward. She walked around the edge of the group and took a place near a crooked oak tree. She sat down on one of the bare roots of the tree.

Cynthia Ann thought about the way Old Woman could make her sorry if she didn't mind. She was afraid of the woman, but she felt more fear of the chief and the men who followed him into battle.

The white men walked toward Cynthia Ann, speaking with kind voices. They hoped to quiet her fears and to show her that she should go back to her own people. She just sat there without trying to answer them.

When they spoke of her parents and playmates, she did not understand them. They tried everything they could to bring out some feeling or answer from her. They asked her what she would like them to tell her family. They talked about her playmates. She just shook her head sadly. The men took this to mean that she was afraid to answer them. They thought that she had been warned to say nothing to let them know how she really felt. Her lips moved, but she didn't make any answer.

One of the men decided to try again. "Listen, little girl, you have a mother, a brother, and a little sister who love you. They need you at home."

Finally, the chief who had allowed this attempt to talk with her told the men that they might as well go on back. It was hopeless, and after all, not all the goods the men had could buy her.

Colonel Williams and his two companions saw that the Indians did not intend to give her up. Probably, she did not even understand what they were talking about.

"Come on, you two. We might as well leave her here with these savages. She has become one of them," said Colonel Williams. Sadly, the three men made their way out of the Comanche camp. They rode along the Canadian river. After all, three men could not be expected to fight an entire Comanche tribe.

After watching the men leave, the chief spoke kindly to Cynthia Ann, telling her to go back to Old Woman and the children. She went gladly because their play was what she knew best. She wanted to get away from all the talking. She welcomed the shouts of the other children. At least, their teasing was easy to listen to. She didn't have to protect herself or to answer them.

As the months dragged on, she learned to follow the ways and language of the Comanches. They liked her. She was one of them. She had a name now. She didn't have to go on as one who was too scared to speak. They called her "Preloch." It seemed to fit her very well. There was no memory of that other name, Cynthia Ann. It was gone with all the other things from her past. She had forgotten them.

While the years rolled by, Preloch began to take on the charms of a young woman. With her companions, she did the lowly duties of hard work which Indian custom gave to the women. It seemed natural, not cruel. Her life became rather pleasant to her, in spite of all the hard work. The Comanche braves gave all the hard work to women. The only chore which the Indian brave performed was that of making weapons. That was not considered women's work, or perhaps they did not think the women were capable of doing such serious work.

Old Woman told Preloch that she was a special person to the tribe. Her yellow hair, which was tangled and greasy, and her blue eyes made her unlike the other young girls. Many a young warrior's heart was moved by the sight of her. She grew slim, tall, and straight. The young men often brought her gifts of game that they took after a long hard chase through Antelope Hills. Shyly, she thanked them for their gifts.

But there was one young man who was more interested than the others. Old Woman told Preloch that he wanted her for his wife. She was afraid of this tall, silent man. She would always be a little fearful of this man who was a war chief of the Quahadi Comanches.

However, he treated her more kindly than the others did. He had stopped shouting at her, the way other people did. Sometimes, he brought her gifts. She liked the bright beads and pretty feathers. She sewed them on her clothing, and she tanned the antelope hide which he had brought to her. This hide would make a pretty dress for her after she and Old Woman could finish tanning it.

That Peta Nocona was serious in his courting

7

would soon be made clear to all the tribe. He began selecting a special herd of horses. He fed them, groomed them, and treated them very carefully. Everyone knew that he was planning a marriage. This marriage could only take place after he had won the consent of Old Woman and her husband, Cynthia Ann's guardians. The husband of Old Woman was the person Nocona would have to show. Nocona laid his plans very carefully.

When the herd was ready, he dressed himself in his best clothes. He tied the herd of ten beautiful horses together and led them to the tepee of Old Woman and her husband. There he tied the horses in front of the tepee and then silently rode back to his own tepee.

Since the weather was sharp and cool, he stood just inside the opening of the tepee and watched the herd of horses. He was eager to know what effect his gift would have on Preloch's family. If the old man accepted them, then he could proceed to make further plans. With the fall hunting season upon them, it would be easy to supply the old man and woman with plenty of meat for the winter. He was sure that this was one demand they would make upon him. He would just have to work a little harder, but he would have Preloch's help in preparing and drying the meat.

He had no doubt about Preloch's feelings. She had already accepted the small gifts that he had brought her. She always smiled when she thanked him for his gifts. He knew she would not oppose his plan.

Preloch watched the events with great interest. She knew about the custom of making a gift to ask for a wife. She also knew that Nocona had placed one of

his best ponies in the lead position. The gift of this pony meant that he was very serious about his plan to make her his wife. No Comanche would ever give away his favorite horse without good reason.

Preloch thought what it would mean to be the wife of a Great Chief. At last, her future would be safe. She would have a high place as Nocona's chosen wife. Since he had taken no other wives, it meant that she would be in charge of his home. She did hope that the old man would accept this gift from Nocona. She knew that the old people liked her, even though Old Woman was often hard on her. They would want a good life for her, she knew. Then Preloch heard a sound inside the tepee of Old Woman.

The old man came out of the tepee. He took the lead horse by the leather rein. He led the horses toward the spot where he kept his own horses. A touch of a smile curled the lip of Nocona. At last, the yellow-haired girl would be his. He would waste no time in making his visit to the old man. Nocona was ready to promise anything he might ask. Preloch was worth anything Old Man might ask.

It was morning. Preloch stretched lazily and watched the sun change the leaves from dark blowing shapes to shining silver and gold. Old Woman shouted at her. She knew this day was to be nice. This was the day when Nocona would come to claim her as his wife.

She rose slowly from her bed of sweet smelling grass. First, she would bathe in the chilly, cold water in the creek before the others rose. Then as Old Woman had told her, she must put on the antelope hide dress. It was as soft and fine as silk. Old Woman had helped her to make the dress. For weeks they had scraped and chewed the leather. They had cut the hem into a deep fringe. The sides were fringed with a short cut.

Preloch braided her wet hair into two long braids. The beads had been sewn into a band for her hair. With the pretty eagle feather tucked into the band, she would be dressed for Nocona to come for her.

She saw Old Woman moving around the morning fire. Preloch moved toward the welcome warmth of the early fire. She would move into Nocona's tepee. As the first wife of a great chief, no one would ever shout at her again.

Preloch ate her morning meal. She was not really hungry. She ate only a few nuts and some dried meat, which had been seasoned with berries. These she washed down with a long drink of water from the creek. She heard a soft noise above her. She looked up from the creek bank.

The great chief Nocona stood quietly outside the Old Woman's tepee. He had come for his bride. Old Woman went out to call Preloch. She took the girl's hand in her own and led her to Nocona. He nodded silently at the shy girl. Old Woman placed Preloch's hand in Nocona's hand. He led her away from Old Woman. The young girl, who in her past life might have had a beautiful church wedding, was content with this simple wedding of her Indian family.

The story of Cynthia Ann Parker had begun many years before her capture by the Comanches of Texas. It was in Virginia that the story first started with the wedding of her grandfather, Elder John Parker, to Sally White, the girl who had waited for him through the Revolutionary War. John and Sally were married in Virginia, where three of their six sons were born. The family moved south to Georgia, where another son was born. Then they chose to go west over the mountains to Tennessee. It was in Tennessee that Cynthia Ann's father, Silas, and the youngest son, Benjamin, were born.

Before very long the family decided to move further north to Illinois. While in Illinois, Silas and James Parker married two sisters, who were Lucy and Martha Duty. It was also in Illinois that Cynthia Ann Parker was born. She was the oldest child of Silas and Lucy Parker. Her beloved little brother, John, was born three years later.

The children were brought up in a strict, Baptist manner. John Parker had been named an elder in the church. Thus he was called "Elder John" by the members of his church. When it was decided that the group would move to Texas, Elder John formed his own church group.

It was against the laws of Texas at that time to have a Baptist church there. Texas was still under the rule of Mexico in the early 1830's, and Mexico accepted only those persons of Catholic faith. The religious group to which the Parkers belonged were good, hard-working people who believed that their efforts and strict beliefs would lead them to heaven. They doubted any other way to the heavenly reward which they sought. Therefore they could not accept the Catholic faith that Mexico would have required of them.

The Parker family was one that remained together. When the grandfather decided that they should move, the entire family, children and grandchildren, packed their belongings to go with him. His sons and their families made a large group for the trip.

Before the entire family left for Texas, it was decided that James and Silas would go ahead of the group. They would decide which part of Texas would be right for their new home. Land was free for the taking there. Each head of the family could claim for his family forty-six thousand acres of land. It was on this free land that Elder John decided his whole family should live.

Among this group of loving family members Cynthia Ann was taken to Texas. She learned early the lessons of traveling by wagon train, the making and breaking of camp. The families traveled in the familiar prairie schooners. It was this type of wagon that carried most of the Americans into the wild, beautiful prairies of Texas.

At night, Cynthia Ann, John, their mother, and the new baby slept in the wagon. Their father and the other men slept under the wagons except when they were on watch. A watch was posted every night to keep the horses and other animals near the wagons. Also, they feared Indian attacks on the way through Missouri.

They made a bed for the little baby in the small trunk which Lucy had been given as a bride. Even when the wagon train was on the move, the baby could take his naps in the trunk near his mother on the spring seat. Lucy and the children made their beds on the quilts which they had brought from Illinois. They were spread over the chests that lined the sides of the wagon bed. It pleased Cynthia Ann to hear her mother describe the double wedding ring pattern of the best quilt. There was another quilt, a Dutch doll pattern, which Cynthia Ann knew that her mother meant her to have when she married.

They had brought only two pieces of furniture with them. Lucy could not give up the rocking chair in which she had nursed both of her babies. Then there was the mahogany chest which Lucy had gotten from her mother's family. These things could not be left behind in Illinois. However, everything else had been sold or given away before they drove off from their home in Illinois.

It really didn't matter about the furniture. All the men in the Parker family had been taught to make furniture. Carving was almost as natural as breathing with them. Silas Parker would make new furniture for the family as soon as they got a house built. His father John had always made the sturdy, well-built pieces that Granny Parker used in their family home. But somehow, Cynthia Ann was glad that they had made room for the rocking chair. It was tied high on one of the hoops that held the canvas covering over the wagon bed.

The boxes and chests that lined the sides of the wagon bed held food, clothing, medicine, and other belongings that were needed for the travelers. Her mother's pots and pans were stored in a box tied on the back of the wagon. At night when they were camped early, a pot of stew or beans could be started at once. Everyone was always hungry after a day of riding over the rough prairie trails. Another item which her mother kept very carefully was the crock of sour dough. When they stopped for a day or two to wait for a swollen creek to go down, Lucy would mix up some new dough for bread. She would add a little pinch of the old dough to make the new bread rise. Then after each new batch was mixed, some of the new dough was added to the sour dough crock. Lucy always had made the best smelling bread in the Parker families. It was always the lightest, sweetest bread in the camp. Everyone was glad when Lucy got out her sour dough crock. They knew supper would be good that night.

For little Cynthia Ann this was a slow-moving, happy time. The every day routine of making and breaking camp was a joyous time for her. She crawled happily out of the wagon and ran over the new camp site, visiting with all the other travelers. She especially liked to visit with her Granny Parker, who could be counted on to have a left-over cookie or biscuit for her and John.

The tired and travel-worn grown-ups found it a time of worry and hard work. The wagon train crossed the Mississippi river at St. Louis, Missouri. There they had purchased supplies needed for the long trip ahead. This would be the last time that they would pass a city of any size for many long days.

The cattle and wagons were taken across the river on large flat boats. Cynthia Ann watched as they loaded the wagons on the flat boats. The river looked so wide and so muddy that it frightened her. She feared the boats would sink or that the wagons would slip off the boats. She stood beside her mother, who was holding the baby. They could feel the boat slipping through the fast moving water. It didn't look fast, but the movements of the boat made her know that it was fast. They had already taken the oxen, the horses, and the cattle across. The men who worked the boats were very fast and careful. They had an easy way of working that gave Cynthia Ann a little more secure feeling.

The family would make it across. She knew that, but it was still frightening. By nightfall, all the wagons and the travelers were across the river. They checked everything for an early start the next morning.

From this time the wagon train followed the Mississippi river south. Crossing the smaller streams that poured into the great, muddy Mississippi often presented risks. Many times the party traveled miles out of the way just to cross a flooded river. Sometimes the river banks were so high that it was hard to pass.

However, the grassy flats of Missouri were a joy to the children. At times Cynthia Ann hated to leave a very beautiful spot among the trees. The trip across Arkansas became more difficult. There were more rivers and rough country to cross.

Early one evening they finally found a smooth spot near a rushing river for their night's supper. Silas and James had seen some deer a short distance away. With luck, they could have fresh deer meat that night. The men could skin and dress a deer very quickly. There would be plenty of meat for a day or two. While the women were busy with the setting up of camp, the older boys in the group would try their luck at fishing. Perhaps they would get a few trout.

"Mama, may I have some of the dough?" asked Cynthia Ann. She had set up her own little household under the wagon. She placed her doll in the shade of the water barrel attached to the side of the wagon.

"Of course, child. Just don't try to eat the raw dough," answered her mother. "It isn't good for you."

While the men were hunting the wild game, the women had hurriedly made make-shift ovens over piles of rocks so that they could bake bread to last for several days. In fact, one reason they had stopped early today was that they needed to add to their supply of fresh food. They could cook beans that had been soaking all day in the pots stored in the wagons, bake the fresh bread, and cook enough of the meat to last them for quite awhile.

With a little searching along the river, they just might find enough wild berries to make a cobbler. A little syrup with the berries could make a very tasty pie. Cynthia Ann and her cousins had hunted among the trees and bushes while the women worked over the fires. Her older cousins picked several baskets of the rosy berries. It seemed that supper tonight would be extra special. Maybe there would be singing of the old hymns afterwards.

Cynthia Ann hummed a little song as she busied herself building a rock oven. She pinched the small piece of dough into little loaves to rise in the old jar lid that she carried in her toy box. Tomorrow while they were riding in the wagon, Lucy had promised Cynthia Ann that she would find some scraps of material and teach her to cut out the pieces for a double wedding ring quilt. She could piece a little quilt to cover the doll bed that Silas had promised to make for her.

The days became longer and longer. Texas must be such a long distance away. It seemed they would never reach the river where James and Silas had told them that they would build their new homes.

The day was Saturday and the wagon train was preparing to stop for the special Sunday services. Elder John always enjoyed the weekend rest more than any other part of the trip. It meant that the entire day would be spent in rest and in worship. All the cooking and other preparations must be made on Saturday afternoon so that their entire attention could be given over to the day-long worship services and hymn singing. No work, not even cooking, could be done on the Sabbath.

Cynthia Ann was allowed to play on Saturday afternoon, but on Sunday even the little children were expected to spend the day in worship. They did not play nor sing, except for the old familiar hymns. The horses were tied so that they could graze, as were the other cattle. No one could spend any time in any sort of work. The Sundays seemed very long to the young children. Cynthia Ann liked Sunday, but she was always glad when Monday morning brought about action and movement.

The moving took a long time, and the trail to Texas became harder for the tired travelers. Throughout Missouri there had been the worry of Indian raids, but the fear that they had felt there was nothing to compare with the stories that made them worry when they heard about the Indians in Texas. The very word *Comanche* caused even Elder John to shake with fear.

Slowly the wagon train moved down the countryside toward Logansport. Here they were forced to wait for the Sabine river to go down so that they could cross. There was a ferry that would take them across the river when it was safe. From there they were to take a trail that was called the Coushatta Trace, which had been made by the Coushatta Indians in their travels and trading.

After crossing on the ferry, the family kept moving southwest toward the Angelina river. The Angelina crossing was soon followed by the crossing of the Neches river. Then it was the Trinity river that slowed them down. They were traveling very slowly because there were no roads southwest through the Coushatta Indian territory. It seemed to Cynthia Ann and John that they might never reach their new home.

When they arrived in the southwestern part of what is today Grimes County, they set up camp to remain until the men could build their new homes. They remained in Grimes County for over a year. Here they found life a little easier than the traveling had been. There was a post office, a gin, and a stage stop to remind them of their past life.

It was during this time that James and Silas Parker, and Elisha Anglin, another settler, set out for the northwest where they hoped to find good land for their new homes. They had seen rich, black prairie land and many streams in the area. There was plenty of wild game and the fishing was good in the rushing streams.

It was during this time in Grimes county that a new child was born to the Silas Parker family. Now Cynthia Ann and John had a little sister, in addition to Silas, Jr., the little brother who had been born just before the trip started. The women and children waited for the men to return from their search for just the right land for their claims.

Silas and James Parker placed claims for land north of the present town of Groesbeck in Limestone

County. It was beautiful, rich country near the Navasota River. Although it was further west than some of the wagon train wanted to go, it seemed to be the best choice for James and Silas.

From Grimes County, the wagon train of Parker families made its way up the east side of the Navasota river until they reached the old San Antonio Road. This was the road which the Spanish had used in traveling from San Antonio to the east Texas town of Nacogdoches. The wagons then continued toward the northwest until they reached Fort Sam Houston, which was located about two miles west of the present city of Palestine. It was the early spring of 1834. They had been on the road from Illinois for about two and a half years now. They were glad to see the half dozen cabins that had been built around the fort's walls. Here they rested before recrossing the Trinity river toward Limestone County.

They traveled about forty-five miles before they reached the rich, dark land which Silas and James had chosen for their homes. In the spring of 1834 the brothers, Silas, James, and Benjamin, with the aid of several others, built Parker's Fort, which was a kind of wooden wall built around their cabins. This wall would give them safety from the warlike Indians who roamed the countryside. About ten families lived at Parker's Fort, with Elder John as their leader.

The fort was about the size of a present day football field. It had a large double gate which opened to the inside of the fort. The outer walls of the log cabins formed a part of the walls of the stockade. Their roofs dropped inward. At two of the corners of the fort guard houses were built above the fence. They ran out about three feet beyond the walls, thus giving the guards a full view of all four sides of the fort. There

were holes all around the inside of the fence from which guns could be fired. The fort was built so that the few men could hold off any Indian raid by a well-armed and careful group of settlers. A clearing in the woods around the fort kept the Indians from making any surprise attacks.

Cynthia Ann and John watched for hours as the men cut down the huge trees and dragged them into position for the cabins and walls. While this work was going on, they still lived in the covered wagons that had carried them so far. They had to play near the fort because the parents were busy and could not watch after them if they strayed away.

The elders were worried not only about the Indians, but also about the outcome of the war with Mexico. If the "Tejanos," as the Indians called them, won the war, they would be free to build their own church here at Parker's Fort. There was one fearful time when they were forced to flee from the Mexican army's advance. In the spring of 1836 they were in the "run-away scrape," fleeing as far east as the Trinity river on their way to Fort Houston. Because the river was swollen by heavy rains, they were unable to cross. They were camped on the western bank when they heard about the victory at San Jacinto. At once they packed and moved back to their homes at Fort Parker.

When they reached home, they began at once to gather their scattered stock and to prepare the fields for planting. They had cleared fields near the Navasota river away from the fort. Cynthia Ann and John played happily just outside the gates of the fort. Life was finally settling down for everyone, and they lived with expectation of a calm, happy future. It seemed that nothing could harm them now. They were well protected in their new homes. Lucy Parker often sat and shucked corn or shelled beans while she watched her children at play. Some of the men went every day to work the fields about a mile from the fort.

# 3. The Massacre at Fort Parker

Soft May breezes blew up little clouds of dust. The gentle scent of Texas bluebonnets filled the air. It was cool in the morning shade of the stockade. Two children played quietly just outside the open gates. Usually, the gates were closed, but today was such a perfect day that the children were allowed to build playhouses on the outside without their mother's usual warnings.

It was May 19, 1836, at a spot near the Navasota River, close to the present day town of Groesbeck. Inside the gates of Parker's Fort, two women worked over tubs of hot, sudsy water and rub boards. They were scrubbing dust and grime from the families' clothing.

The little girl, Cynthia Ann Parker, nursed the corn husk baby which her father had made for her the night before. She held it tenderly in her arms as she crooned to it. She had carefully piled rocks around her playhouse. She could make-believe that these two rooms were her own home.

John, her brother, was busily digging a garden to feed his make-believe family. Happily, he thought of the early poke salet which the men might bring home that night. The winter had been a long, hard one. Fresh vegetables would taste very good. The thought made his mouth water. He could almost taste the cornbread and poke salet greens. His father had said that they might find some growing wild along the creek bank.

Cynthia Ann's mother Lucy called out to a neighbor. She had made an extra pie for their supper.

The two women at the rub boards looked up. They smiled happily at the thought of the hot pies. The berries in the woods were plump and juicy this spring.

No one paid any attention to the clouds of dust arising on the southern edge of the clearing. Had they noticed, they would have thought perhaps it was only another visitor. Visitors often dropped by for a meal with the Parker families.

Elder John, Cynthia Ann's grandfather, sat under a small oak tree inside the stockade. He was carving on a stubby branch which he had broken from a lower limb of the tree. Elder John was very clever with his knife. He had learned this work when he was only a boy in Virginia. His wife, Granny Parker, smiled. She thought of how happy he was with this new life in Texas.

Silas and Benjamin, two of Elder John's sons, worked at the forge. Silas was making a new horseshoe. He had removed one from his brother's horse just that morning. He wanted to have it ready when his brother James returned from the fields that evening.

Only six men had been left to protect the fort. The others were either at their own cabins away from the fort or were working their fields near the Navasota river. There were about ten women and fifteen children in the settlement. It was truly a happy time for the families. Spring was here. There had not been reports of Indians for days. None had been seen anywhere near the fort.

The clouds on the western edge of the woods began to grow larger. Granny Parker, who had walked out to watch Cynthia Ann and John at their play, looked up at the sky. Noticing the clouds, she put her hand to shade her old eyes from the bright morning sun.

Granny shouted to her son, Ben. Who could be making such a stir of dust? Ben took only one look. Then he shouted quickly to the playing children. Indians! The children knew the dreaded word well. They knew what to do. They sprang up from their play and dashed inside the fort. Mrs. Parker ran to her two children to hurry them toward the back of the fort, where her other two children were sleeping.

It might be a war party from the speed with which they were riding. Ben and Silas started pushing on the heavy folding gates to the stockade. Elder John dropped his carving and started running toward the gate. Although he was a man of some seventy years, he still ran spryly.

Hurriedly, the other men began climbing to the lookout tower on the south side of the fort. They picked up their already loaded muskets. Granny ran to fill the buckets with water from the wash tubs. She would be ready for any burning arrows they might send. Granny Parker was a woman of great courage.

It was nine o'clock when they saw the first riders among the hundreds of horsemen approaching the gates. Some five to seven hundred Indians, both Comanche and Kiowa, appeared on the prairie two or three hundred yards from the fort. They displayed a dirty white flag. One of the leaders rode toward the gate where Silas and Ben were standing.

Cynthia Ann and John tried to peer from behind Silas's legs. Cynthia Ann whimpered in fear. Mrs. Parker put her arms around them, trying to lead them away from the sight.

"Come, come, children," she said. "We must look after the babies."

Ben turned to his brother Silas. "They just want to talk," said Ben. "Perhaps I had better go out to meet them. It won't do to let them get too close."

Silas was not convinced that Ben should take such a chance with his life. "I don't think you should try it, Ben," he replied. "Let's get these gates closed and locked. We can keep them out, at least for a while."

"Well," drawled Ben, "we'll never know if I don't go out. Maybe they just want some water or some food." He wasn't really fooling himself. Food was plentiful on the prairie during the spring.

Elder John heard his boys talking. He started waving to Ben to wait. The boys knew that Elder John would want to talk to the Indians himself. Elder John thought it was his duty to protect these people whom he had led to this wild part of Texas.

"I'll go before he gets here," Ben said quickly to Silas. "He'll never agree to let me go. He'll want to go himself."

Silas stepped back to stop his father. Ben walked outside toward the approaching Indian. The two children and Mrs. Parker stood frozen with fear. She hugged her two children to her. They watched in panic as Ben approached the Indian.

"Mama! Look at them! They're naked," cried Cynthia Ann in horror. She held tightly to her mother's skirts as Mrs. Parker hurried them swiftly toward their own cabin.

Ben walked firmly out toward the Indian. The other Indians were moving closer and closer to the fort. They stopped at the sound of Ben's voice. He spoke briefly with the leader.

Silas could see Ben shaking his head, but he could not make out what Ben was saying. He wondered what they would ask for this time. Sometimes they had had a few Indians come by to request food or water. But this time it was spring. There was plenty of water in the river. Deer and other small animals were easy to catch. The Indians couldn't be hungry.

As Silas watched, Ben turned and walked back to the fort. He spoke briefly with Silas. Then he moved inside to talk with his father. The Indians waited in silence.

"The chief said that they want a beef," Ben told Silas and his father.

Cynthia Ann and John held their mother's long skirt tightly as they walked back toward the cabin. She placed an arm around each of them. She hoped that these Indian visitors would be friendly. Cynthia Ann was terribly frightened. She had heard the stories about Indian raids. She did hope that her uncle Ben could make them go away. Surely he could make the Indians leave.

Silas and Ben knew that their father would not agree to give the Indians a beef. The settlers were already short of meat. They had lost two cows just this spring. They couldn't give up another now.

"I guess we'll just have to give them the young calf," said Benjamin.

Silas thought a minute, and then he replied, "Ben, you know that won't satisfy them. Besides that, Pa won't agree to that."

The Indian outside the gate was watching the men intently. He was conscious of the small number of men he could see at the fort.

"It would be easy," he thought to himself, "to

27

take these 'Tejanos' by surprise." He kept watching
the two men at the inside door of the fort. They
couldn't seem to make up their minds. Well, he and
his followers would make them up soon enough!!

Ben turned to go back outside. Silas was telling
him not to go. Silas tried to close the gate in front of
Ben.

"Ben, you know they'll kill you," said Silas.

Ben answered shortly, "I don't have any other
choice. Perhaps they'll take some of the corn meal.
Tell Ma to get some baskets of food ready."

He really knew better than that. The Indians had
always refused to take corn meal. They just fed the
dried meal to their horses. They made fun of the
whites for eating such food.

Ben was approaching the Indian rider again. The
others kept moving in closer to the gate. When they
met, Ben shook his head in refusal. Silas tried hard to
hear what they were saying to Ben.

Suddenly, one of the braves shouted a piercing
scream. He lunged toward Ben with his lance. Ben
fell to the ground. The lance pinned him there. The
nearest Indian dashed inside the fort through the
open gate. Silas and Elder John watched in horror.
There was no time to close the gates now.

While the tragedy was in progress, Elder John
Parker, "Granny" Parker, and Mrs. Kellogg fled
through a side door in the fort. Lucy Parker and her
children escaped through a back door. Silas Parker
and Mrs. Plummer ran out through the gate.
Everyone was trying to escape the savage attack. Mrs.
Sarah Nixon had run toward the farm to warn the
others of the attack by the Indians. Somehow she had
gotten away without being seen.

Most of the Indians rushed through the open gate of the fort. However, some of them went after those who were trying to flee out the back door. The Indians shouted and yelled while they were murdering Ben Parker. It was a bloody sight and horrible screams rose above the noise of the fight. The listeners would never forget this sound—the Comanche war cry.

Mrs. Parker had hurried the children toward the river back of the fort. Just as the first group of Indians had dashed inside the stockade, she pushed her children ahead of her and ran after them.

Several of the Indians had expected just such a move. As the frightened mother and her children fled toward the river, they were caught by shouting, yelling Indians. With his lance at her heart, one of the Indians forced Mrs. Parker to put Cynthia Ann behind him on his horse and to put John behind another savage.

Cynthia Ann screamed for her mother. John held on to the back of the Indian who had taken him.

"Mama! Mama!" shouted Cynthia Ann.

About that time one of the men from the fields came running up to the screaming, fighting group. He grabbed Mrs. Parker and two of her children, pushing them away from the Indians. He raised his musket to fire on them. The Indians left Mrs. Parker and the younger children, racing away with their two young captives, John and Cynthia Ann.

Mrs. Parker and her two children were pushed toward the grove of trees near the river. There they hid with several of the others who had climbed through a hole in the back of one of the cabins.

29

Meanwhile, inside the fort the Indians were murdering and scalping Silas Parker, Samuel and Robert Frost. Elder John Parker, "Granny" Parker, and Mrs. Kellogg were captured before they got to the creek. They were brought back to the fort, where Elder John was killed and mutilated. "Granny" Parker was speared and left for dead. Mrs. Kellogg was taken away as a prisoner.

When it was all over, the Indians had killed five men. Then they plundered the entire settlement. They tore through the cabins, destroying everything that they didn't want or couldn't use. They took guns, weapons, food, and anything else they fancied.

Those of the settlement who made it to hiding in the river bottom spent a fearful day and night. At twilight, Abram Anglin and Evan Faulkenberry started back to the fort. It was near Seth Anglin's cabin that they found "Granny" Parker. She had pretended to be dead until after the Indians had left. Then she had started out crawling toward the Anglin cabin, more dead than alive. Abram Anglin thought she was a ghost when he first saw her. He took some bed clothes, made her a bed and covered her up. They left her there until they could go on to the fort to see about the others.

At the fort they didn't find anyone alive. There was no sound of humans, but some of the dogs and pigs could be heard barking and squealing. Since the men found no one alive at the fort, they left without burying the dead. Fearing that the Indians would return, they went back to get "Granny" Parker and returned to the river in a hurry. They made their way back to the hiding place in the river bottom.

Next morning early some of the men went back

to the fort where they found five or six horses, a few saddles, and some food. They hurried back to the hiding place to pick up the other refugees. The party then made its way to Fort Houston about forty-five miles to the east. "Granny" Parker died soon after their arrival at Fort Houston. A party of twelve men went back to the fort to bury the dead that had been left there. Much later, most of the survivors returned to the fort to piece their lives back together and to rebuild their homes.

The Indians felt sure that punishment would be swift. So when they had finished their evil work, they rode swiftly toward the northwest. They knew that the white men would be slow to follow them into this wild, unsettled area. They traveled together until midnight. Then they stopped, went into camp, and tied their prisoners so tightly hand and foot that blood welled up into their faces. The Indians built fires, erected a pole, and then engaged in a scalp dance that lasted until morning.

During the dance, they played over the murders that they had done until all of them were so tired that they had to rest. They leaped into the air, shouting and chanting themselves hoarse. They kicked the prisoners and beat them until they lay in fear upon the ground. Blood covered their bodies. When the dance was over, the prisoners, Mrs. Kellogg, Mrs. Plummer, and the children, were more dead than alive.

When the Indians parted company to go their own ways, the prisoners were divided among the tribes. Mrs. Plummer was taken away from her son, James. He was taken by one band; she, by another.

Mrs. Kellogg was sold to another tribe. Later, Mrs. Kellogg was brought to General Sam Houston, who paid the Indians $150 for her.

Mrs. Plummer suffered horrible treatment before she was finally ransomed from the Indians by Mr. William Donoho, a merchant and trader from Santa Fe. Mr. and Mrs. Donoho took her back to her father-in-law's home in Independence, Missouri. From there she traveled to her father's home in Texas. It had been almost four years since she was captured at Parker's Fort. Cynthia Ann and John Parker were taken by different tribes of Comanches into the northern part of Texas.

# 4. Comanche Wife and Mother

The years passed slowly after the raid on Fort Parker. During the long days Cynthia Ann had grown from a child of nine to a young lady. Her childhood behind her, she was now the wife of Nocona, the great chief of the Quahadi Comanches. The past had faded from her memory. She could barely remember her life with her white family. It was just a dim blur. She was an Indian now, content with her lot, even liking it at times.

A few weeks after the marriage of Nocona and Preloch, the tribe began preparing for its fall buffalo hunt. The Comanches always had their annual hunt soon after the first deep frost. The buffalo had moved south on the plains for the winter, and that was the time when the Comanches prepared for the cold winter spell. They must provide enough food and shelter against the long, cold months of Texas winter.

The scouts had already been sent out to pick the best spot for their fall buffalo hunt. They always watched for flocks of ravens which would point out the buffalo herds. The ravens fed on insects that were on the buffaloes. There were so many buffalo on the plains that year that it was only necessary that the Indians pick a spot near water and timber. There was always great excitement when it was time for the hunting season. All the able-bodied men and women and the older children were allowed to go with the hunting party. The scouts went ahead of the tribe to erect the drying scaffolds for the buffalo kill. Everyone did his part in the work of preparing for the winter.

Preloch and the other women with the older youths would pack the hunting tents and other equipment. The hunting tent was always a buffalo skin or two that could be thrown over a pole supported by crossed stakes. This shelter would protect them from unexpected cold weather or rain. The two poles were tied together behind mules or pack horses, with a buffalo skin stretching from one pole to the other. This skin, or travois, held all the food and tools which were necessary to the hunt.

Old Woman and her husband had taken Preloch with them on many buffalo hunts. It was not new to Preloch, except that this time she had to prepare well for Nocona's hunt camp. She must not forget the necessary tools to scrape and cure the skins. There must be bone knives to slice the meat into long, thin pieces so that it will dry well. After all the needed items had been gathered, they must be packed to fit on a travois so that they can be hauled to the spot picked for the hunt.

This part was only the beginning of the work of getting ready for winter weather. But Preloch looked forward to the dances that preceded the trip. Sometimes even as many as two or three nights were spent in fun and dancing before the hunt. This would be Preloch's first hunt dance as the wife of a chief. Preloch would dress in her best dress and paint her face carefully so that she would be pleasing to her new husband.

Old Woman had taught her to put the red and yellow paint around her eyelids, and to paint on the bright red spots on her cheeks. Her ears had to be painted inside with red paint. Since she was now a wife, her long hair had been cropped short. She

parted it in the middle and colored the part line with
bright red paint.

Preloch now had a deer skin dress, soft and
pretty, in a muted lemon yellow color that almost
matched her hair. She had made the skirt from two
deer hides, with the sides sewn up with buckskin
thongs. The edges were fringed before they were
sewed together. The bottom of the dress was deeply

fringed, almost to her knees. Her blouse was made from a single skin, with a long slit in the skin for the neckline. It too was deeply fringed all around the edges, and it was laced together at her waist with buckskin strips. Preloch had sewed beads just above the hemline fringe and around the neckline. A collar was beaded in front where it hung from her slender throat, and on the back it contained signs of the war honors that her husband had won. Nocona was a great chief; thus Preloch's collar had many figures on it.

On her feet, Preloch wore beautiful, beaded moccasins. For the dance tonight she decided not to wear her leggings. It was not cold enough yet to demand the wearing of extra clothing. The dancing would be enough to keep Preloch warm this night.

When Preloch came out of the tepee, she saw that the bright fire had already been lit. She was glad because dancing in the firelight was fun. Sometimes when there was a full moon, the hunt party did not even bother with a fire. But Preloch liked the fun of smelling and watching the burning wood. Autumn was such a nice season. The fire crackled and sparked as the excited dancers circled around it.

The men had lined up, and the women now faced them. When the singing and the drums began, the women crossed over to pick out a partner. Preloch moved like an arrow toward waiting Nocona. Their dance had begun. Preloch liked the freedom of being able to dance with the elders and to choose her partner as she had seen others do many times in the past. The dancing and singing became more active as the night went on. It lasted until the last dancer had dropped, worn out by the dance. It was after midnight when Preloch and Nocona finally went toward their tepee. It had been a good dance and the hunt promised to be good this year. There would be plenty of meat for the People.

The next morning they arose to the great fun of the hunt. The runners had returned from picking out the hunting spot for this year. Preloch was happy when she learned that it was to be Palo Duro Canyon. The runners said that there were hundreds of buffalo there just waiting for the hunters. It would indeed be a good hunt this year.

In the fall of the year, Palo Duro Canyon was beautiful with its trees clothed in red and gold. The tall stately cottonwoods had turned to many different hues after the frost had hit them. This was a perfect time for camping out under the stars with a warm buffalo robe for the chillier nights.

The packing now began in earnest. The travois had to be tied to the pack horses and mules, and then they must be loaded with all the needed supplies. Preloch had her own little pinto pony that she would ride. The children who would be left with the older Comanches were crowding around, begging to be taken on one of the travois. But this was no time for children, as much as their parents loved them. This was a busy time of work and sweat. They could not be watching children while they were killing and dressing the buffalo.

The hunt chief checked all the families, to be sure that they were ready for the long trek to Palo Duro. Then he gave the sign that started the long parade of dancing horses, slow-moving pack horses with the travois, and the women seated on their own mounts in the rear. The children laughed and shouted with glee as the train pulled out toward the northwest. At long last, the time had come for the hunt.

It was near sunset of the fourth day when they pulled out just above the chosen place. The long, narrow valley cut by many deep ditches provided a natural spot for the kill. They camped down wind from the large herd of buffalo, which they could see from the canyon wall. Tonight they would eat and rest. Tomorrow the work would really begin. The pack horses and mules were unhitched from their burdens. They were tied to graze in a small meadow where the grass was lush and brown.

Preloch unpacked some of the food which she had prepared for them to eat. Nocona sat down and leaned against a wind-bent mesquite tree, while he chewed slowly on the pemmican that Preloch had offered him. It seemed that Preloch knew more about making pemmican than anyone else he had ever known. Old Woman must have taught her well. She had taken the strips of meat, pounded it well, and dried it in the sun. Then she had packed it in pecans which had been pounded into a powder. Finally, she had poured tallow over the mixture. It was the candy that all Comanche children begged for. Nocona liked the sweet taste that it left in his mouth.

Preloch slowly chewed on a strip of the dried meat while she gazed out over the herd of buffalo watering along the river that ran from west to east through the canyon. Tomorrow would be a hard day for her because this year she had to see that Nocona's store of meat for the winter was correctly prepared. There were no fires tonight because of the nearness of the buffalo. Tonight they would just curl up to sleep at dusk.

In the morning at the first sign of light over the

horizon, the entire hunting camp arose and prepared for the work of the day. There was plenty of hard work for all, but the fun of the hunting camp came in the form of great feasts and dancing after all the work was done.

The hunt chief directed the work of the morning. The hunters were not very quiet because the buffalo depended upon his sense of smell for warning. He couldn't see very well because of the long hair and fur that he grew in the winter time. He couldn't hear very well either. Thus his nose gave him the best clues to danger.

Moving up into position against the wind in a great semi-circle, the Comanche hunters waited patiently for the hunt leader's signal to charge into the valley. When the signal was given, they began to close in the circle that they were forming. They circled around and around the herd until they had them moved into a great mass. The buffalo on the outside of the mass provided a good target for the Indians' arrows and lances. The killing of the buffalo was a very easy task. There were so many animals that the few who escaped were not even chased.

Buffalo hunting was exciting to the Comanche rider. It was a time of winning. There were plenty of buffalo; so there was no quarrel about who killed each animal. The lances and arrows of each hunter were marked so that the owner was easily known. If there should arise a problem, it was usually the custom to give that buffalo to the old men of the tribe, who could not hunt for themselves any more.

After the killing was over, the real work of the hunt began. Nocona and the other men did the heavy work of skinning and cutting up the animals. They worked fast while the meat was fresh. As soon as they finished with an animal, Preloch and the other women took over their work to bag the meat in hides. They packed it on the mules and pack horses to carry it back to the hunt camp. There they would further process the meat. As soon as they had all of the meat packed and loaded, the women drove the pack animals back to the camp.

When they reached the camp, the men lay down to rest while the women drove the pack animals close to the drying racks. Preloch sliced the meat from Nocona's buffalo into very thin strips which she then hung over the racks in the sun. While the men were busy shooting, the women had carefully checked the drying racks to see that they were ready. After a day or two the meat would be ready to take back to the home camp.

After the meat was hung on the racks, Preloch and her fellow workers put the hides out on the ground. With one worker holding the hide with the flesh side out, the others drove sticks into the ground to stretch the hide as it dried. This way some of the work of tanning would already be done when they reached their home.

When the hunt party had returned to the home camp, they were ready to prepare themselves for their annual move into the upper hill country of Texas. Somewhere down the Colorado River they would find a warm spot where they could winter without too much trouble from the white hunters or soldiers.

Winters were a time of her life that Preloch liked. Usually, these were quiet times. The men would not be thinking about raids until springtime. Or perhaps if they ran out of food because the winter was longer or harder than usual, they might hunt out a white settlement. They might be forced to take meat or food from the white man. Preloch dreaded the worry that the raids brought. She feared for the life of Nocona, although as a good wife, she did not show the fear that she felt.

Also, moving south meant that the tribe would be in a fresh new place. Preloch could find a clean, nice spot for Nocona's tepee. It would be nice to have a cool, fast-running steam beside the tepee. The hill country was not so cold as the northern plains country. There would be bright, cold days with the sun shining warmly in the protected places. There would be time, before the snows came, to pick the rich, oily pecans, the walnuts, the persimmons turned red by the frost, the mesquite seeds that provided sweetening for their food.

Preloch loved the smells that came from the food stored inside the warm tepee. When fires were built, the odor was very inviting. Although Preloch and her people did not like fish, they could make it through the winter on the small game and fish if they had to do so.

Getting ready for the move south was fun. Going to a new place was exciting for all members of the tribe. They made a game of taking down the tepees. Preloch saw that some of the skins were becoming rather worn. But she smiled at the thought that during the long winter days, she would spend her time tanning and preparing the new buffalo hides to take the place of the old ones.

During the trip to the southeast, the tribe camped out without setting up a real camp ground. They traveled during the day time, but camped early enough at night to let the men hunt for antelope and deer. The smaller animals could be skinned and cut up in a short time, and the skins would make good clothing. The fresh meat was also welcome to the tribe. Nuts and fall fruits always made their diet better. These foods were easy to pick along the river as they followed the Colorado to the east and then south.

When they finally located the right spot for the winter camp, it was the duty of the women to set up the camp. That meant unloading the pack animals, unpacking the travois, and helping one another to put up the poles from the travois. These poles would make the frame for their new winter home. The camp location was a pretty one, near the head waters of the Colorado River. Preloch chose a good spot for Nocona's tepee.

Preloch helped some of the other women until it was her turn to make camp, and then they began work on Nocona's tepee. This work was very important to Preloch because this was her first time to set up a winter camp for her husband. She wanted to be certain that everything was just right about this tepee. The poles had to be located just right. They were heavy when she tried to lift them. It took two of the other women to help her hold the twenty-foot pole in place. Still other women grabbed the other three poles and held them in place while Preloch stood on one woman's shoulders as she tied the four poles together.

Then about twenty more poles were placed around the area, spaced evenly between the first four. These poles were carefully tied into place with the first four poles. Some of the women covered their own tepees without bothering to secure them well, but

Preloch was not happy until she had tied each of the poles to stakes which she drove deeply into the ground. This way the wind would not blow Nocona's tepee away during the bad winter storms.

Standing under the poles, Preloch threw up the first of the buffalo coverings to be tied to the poles. They were caught by one of the women who quickly and firmly tied the covering tightly in place. A fold was made in the covering at the top of the tepee. This made a hole through which the smoke could be drawn out of the tepee. The door was made by fastening a buffalo hide across the top of the opening. Preloch sewed a heavy log into the bottom of the covering. This would make sure that the hard winds of winter could not blow in upon the family. This work was done fast, usually taking only about fifteen minutes per tepee.

After Preloch had dug the fire hole in the center of the tepee, she went outside where she dug a ditch all the way around the tepee. This ditch would keep the inside of the tepee dry during the heavy rains and snows. At last she pleased herself with her work. Nocona would be proud of her, she knew. This was a good home.

With the tepee built, it was time for Preloch to move their belongings into the inside. First, she chose two poles about six feet long. These she placed at the back of the tepee, opposite the doorway. She drove stakes inside the poles and tied rawhide strips across the poles to form a bed. After tying these tightly together, she wove longer strips through these, making the rawhide springs. Over his bed she laid the buffalo robes that she had cured for their bedding. As the weather became colder, they would spread the robes over them. Between these warm, furry hides they would sleep snug all winter.

After the bed was completed, Preloch turned her attention to finding and storing a good supply of firewood. Carefully stacked inside the tepee, the wood would make a nice dry place upon which to stack the family's supply of winter food.

While bringing in the new buffalo hides, Preloch thought that by spring she would be ready to cut and fit them for new tepee coverings. She would have to ask Old Woman to help her make the new covers. Together they would plan a party, inviting all the other women to come and help to cut and sew the coverings to fit the tepee. It was difficult work, and Preloch was sure that she could not do it all by herself. They would enjoy very much the day, talking, sewing, and gossiping to their heart's content.

While Preloch worked, Nocona lay in the shade, chewing lazily on the pemmican. He enjoyed seeing his new wife doing her chores. She was good to look at, the way she moved easily while climbing on the shoulders of one of the women to do the tying of the poles. He yawned and stretched himself out on the ground for a nap.

In another time and place, Preloch might have resented this treatment, but it was the expected behavior of the Comanche man. The woman always did the work. That was her job. The men had other important duties. They must protect the women and children, provide food for all the People, and in times of danger, they must stand and fight so that the women and children might escape before they were harmed. Preloch had learned her duties and learned them well. She smiled happily as her gaze fell upon her sleeping husband. Nocona was usually good to her. She enjoyed her life.

Spring comes to the South Plains of Texas in a lovely burst of color and sound. The birds sing merrily. Every morning before the sun rises is a cool quiet reminder of the cool night before. During the spring rains, the land is covered in a growth of wild flowers blooming in the sweet-smelling green grass. The Llano Estacado is covered with shallow lakes that have formed on the desert floor. The beauty is almost breath-taking in its glory. The dry, sunbaked days of later summer are almost forgotten in this rush of spring beauty.

It was just such a spring in 1845 that Preloch and her People arrived at Laguna Sabinas, a salt lake just northwest of the town of Lamesa. It was time to prepare for the birth of a baby to Preloch and Nocona. Their first son was to be born in this beauty of springtime. Preloch had already decided to name her first-born son "Quanah," which means fragrant, sweet-smelling.

According to Comanche custom, Preloch selectd a quiet spot on the far side of the lake. She set up her own tepee there and furnished it with soft, clean buffalo robes. Her son would be born among the glory of the flowers. She carefully prepared his cradle board on which she would carry him to Nocona. Preloch thought of how proud Nocona would be of this, his first son. As was the custom, he would announce to everyone, "I have a good friend!" A son was a very loved possession of the Comanche brave. Nothing could rival the joy that was felt in the birth of a son.

Thus it was with the birth of Quanah Parker,

who would be the most feared warrior of the plains to the white settlers. The name of Quanah was to bring to the white man a feeling of fear that held him back from the lure of the rich lands west of the Trinity River.

In time Preloch gave Nocona another son named Pecos. These two children made up their family until shortly before Preloch was recaptured and taken back to her white people. At that time she had with her a little girl, whom she had named "Prairie Flower."

In the late summer of 1851 Preloch was camped with the tribe somewhere along the upper Canadian river. It was almost time for the fall hunt, and the tribe was making ready to move southward toward the South Plains where they knew that they would find the buffalo herds.

It was about this time that a group of white hunters arrived at the Comanche encampment. They were not there to fight, only to hunt. The Comanches welcomed them in as guests. Preloch eyed the men with fear as she always did white men. She always worried about the safety of her family. Her sons were old enough to ride their ponies alone, and she hurriedly checked to see that they were safe.

While she was running to find the boys, one of the white men noticed her and came closer for a better look. He saw her blue eyes, and quickly he shouted to the others.

"Hey, this here's a white women. No Comanche's got blue eyes!"

Preloch knew that they were talking about her because the man pointed directly toward her. She tried to get out of their sight, but it was of no use. They came toward her. She looked for Nocona, but he was talking with some of the other braves. Preloch trembled under the gaze of the white men.

One of the other men said, "Maybe she's the Parker girl. She's about the right age."

One of the men motioned to Preloch to come with them. She shook her head in a sad manner and put her arms around her young sons. They had come running to her when they saw the white men talking to her. Then, holding her boys back from the strangers, she pointed to Nocona. He stood talking to some of the white men and two braves. His belt was strung with scores of scalp locks.

Preloch spoke to the men in her Comanche tongue.

"I am happy as the wife of the great chief, Peta Nocona. I love my husband, who is kind and good, and my children, who are also his children," she said. "I cannot give up my family."

One of the hunters who spoke Comanche well told the other men what she had said.

As the hunter spoke, Nocona had turned to see the white men talking to his wife. He walked boldly toward the group, at the same time giving Preloch orders to go back to their tepee with the boys. Thus ended one of the many efforts to return Preloch to her white family.

Preloch loved the days when she could sit quietly beside her tepee, watching her two sons play. Nocona took great pride in his sons, but it was Preloch who first started her sons toward the great love of their lives, riding horseback. She took them on her pony with her as soon as they were old enough to be out of the cradle board. They delighted in hanging on to the horses' manes, holding on for dear life as she rode with them through the sand at the edge of the creek.

Quanah especially liked to ride, and he looked forward with eagerness to the day when he could have his own pony. Nocona had promised him one when he reached the age of five. Quanah would not let his father forget that promise. He talked about his pony constantly.

Quanah's father was as eager for his son to ride alone as the son was. Thus on a day in the spring time when Quanah was barely five, Nocona brought to the tepee a beautiful little paint pony.

For some time now Quanah had been riding an old mare that Preloch had given him. He tried to make her run fast, but the poor mare just couldn't please the young lad. There was no way that she could run and turn as swiftly as Quanah wanted her to do.

But with his paint pony Quanah felt as free as a bird. He could almost sail through the air on this new mount. He tried to bring the pony into the tepee with him at night, but his father showed him how to hobble the pony just outside the tepee. In time the pony came to know Quanah as well as he knew the pony. They knew each other well, and the pony obeyed Quanah's every demand. Quanah learned to swing from the pony's neck, riding along while hanging from the pony's side. He could pretend that enemies were waiting to get a shot at him from the far side of the pony. He was very good at this practice, and his father praised him and his riding. Quanah's joy knew no bounds now.

The boys played a game in which they rode in a circle, trying to pick up cow chips from the ground. When Pecos learned to ride and had his own pony, the boys played the game by stacking the chips in a pile. The one with the largest pile at the end of the game was the acting chief during the next game.

Sometimes when Pecos was first learning to ride, Quanah would tie him on the pony. Then holding the pony by a lariat, Quanah would walk the pony in a circle around him. At first, Pecos clung to the pony in fear, but finally after falling a time or two, he learned to hold himself so that he wouldn't fall. He wanted to cry, but he wouldn't let himself because then Quanah would be ashamed of him in front of the other children. Instead, he soon learned to call to Quanah to run the pony faster.

Preloch sat and watched their riding with pride. She knew that Nocona felt the same pride, but he couldn't show it, as she could do. Nocona was just waiting until his sons could join him in the hunts and raids. Then it would be right for him to show the pride that he felt.

About the same time that Quanah was learning to ride, Old Man, his grandfather, started showing him how to make a bow and arrow. He taught Quanah which wood would make the best arrows and which would be best for bows. They hunted for days for just the right kind of flint stone for arrows.

Old Man gave Quanah his first small bow and arrow. It had a dull head on the arrow so that it would not hurt anyone else. Then he taught Quanah to hold the bow and arrow just right and to shoot well. Quanah became as good at this art as he was at riding. It also became second nature to him.

Quanah spent much time in practicing the new arts. He knew that his future life depended upon how good he was at these feats. At first he and Pecos hunted only small birds and rabbits. As they grew older, they went farther and farther from the main camp. Nocona taught his boys to become good hunters. When the boys returned with the birds that they had killed, he praised them highly.

The boys learned to hunt their game with patience, care, and quietness. They learned how to make a surround and how to approach down wind from the animal they hunted. And with all this training, they were also learning about the Comanche's home land. They knew all of its rivers and its creeks, its hills and valleys, and the signs of the prairie. They also knew how to judge the weather, and they knew how to protect themselves from that weather.

Finally, the day came when Nocona took Quanah on his first buffalo hunt. Quanah was so excited that he sat up all night before the hunt. He could not lie down nor rest. He was thrilled with the chance to make his first kill along with the rest of the braves. He could see his first buffalo charging at him as he rode bravely on his pony. He would throw his lance directly at the huge creature's heart.

The next day all his dreams came true. He was the first to break the circle that surrounded the buffalo herd. He circled in toward the milling animals, and he selected his buffalo with care. He wanted the biggest and the fiercest of the animals for his very own. He aimed his lance with great care and then flung it with all the power his arms could make. It went directly toward the buffalo's heart and entered it with deadly force. Quanah's first kill was completed. He was so proud that he almost cried with joy. He finished the day with other successes, but the first kill would always remain in his memory.

That night the entire tribe joined in celebrating Quanah's first hunt. There was wild dancing and singing. He would have another sleepless night because of all the fun. But as it happened, he danced and sang so much, ate so much, that when the party died down, he was more than ready for his buffalo robe and his tepee.

Thus the years passed for Preloch. She was happy in this life, and the happiest times were those when the tribe lived in the Panhandle area of Texas and western Oklahoma along the Canadian River. It was in this vast area that the Comanche found everything that he needed for his life. These animals gave the Comanche food, horn, and hides. The rivers offered wood, forage, fruits, nuts and berries along their banks. The deep canyon breaks provided good protected camp sites.

Preloch and Nocona's family grew larger with the addition of the baby girl whom Preloch named "Prairie Flower." Nocona was not so proud of this girl as he had been of his two sons. Preloch, however, would love her just that much more because Nocona didn't brag about her the way he had about his sons. He said only, "I have a girl."

During this time, Preloch's sons had grown strong and healthy. "Prairie Flower" was still in her cradle board in the spring of 1858. The boys were about ten and twelve years of age.

This spring the tribe had settled along the Canadian River near Antelope Hills of Oklahoma. It was near here that the river made a giant horse-shoe bend as it curved northward and then southward. The area provided as much of a real home for the Comanche as he knew. It was almost a natural fort for him.

There were several different Comanche villages stretched out for miles along the north side of the river. Preloch and Nocona with their children were located in a camp about ten miles above that occupied by "Old Pohebits Quasho," who was the real chief of the Comanches. He had received his nickname of "Iron Jacket" because of the clothing which he wore into battle. This battle dress was that of a Spanish soldier who had probably explored the Southwest as much as three hundred years before this time. The dress included a coat of mail of the type that Coronado or La Salle might have worn in exploring the Southwest. Pohebits Quasho's tribe thought that he could not be harmed when he was dressed in his suit of armor. He had escaped death so many times that the Indians thought that he had cast a spell over his enemies.

On the morning of May 12, 1858, the camp site was quiet except for the barking of a few dogs and the shouting of a group of happy children. Preloch, holding her baby girl Prairie Flower, sat in the shade before her tepee watching her young sons riding and shooting. She was proud of her family, both the boys and her little daughter. Prairie Flower was as pretty as her name suggested. The boys were good in their shooting and riding. Her husband was a subchief of the Comanches, just under Pohebits Quasho. Life was good.

Suddenly, Preloch saw her husband tense his body as he tried to listen to faint sounds in the distance. Immediately, Preloch was aware that something was wrong. Nocona jumped up and raced for his pony, with his lance and bow in his hands. Just then Preloch realized what the sounds were that had disturbed Nocona. They were rifle shots from the enemies' guns. She had heard these sounds before, but this time it seemed as though the sounds didn't end. This was no small raiding party of rangers. It must be a large group of the enemies. Preloch was frightened.

Nocona rode to a high point on the hill directly behind the camp. Swiftly, the other braves armed themselves and gathered around him. They too had recognized the sounds. The young boys, including Pecos and Quanah, were mounted on their ponies. Nocona motioned for them to remain behind with the women. The party of braves grew larger every moment. As they rode toward the sounds, dozens of other Comanches joined the party, until it numbered about five hundred strong.

Preloch, her baby girl strapped on her back, and a few of the younger women from the camp mounted their ponies and followed the warriors at a careful distance. The braves would not approve of their following closely, but the wives knew that they must know what the battle might bring. When they reached a place so that they could see Pohebits Quasho's camp, they hid behind the bushes and rocks so that they would not be seen by the enemy.

Just before they reached the battle scene, a young boy came to tell them that Pohebits Quasho had been slain. The news brought a fear to Nocona, then a sudden pride in the knowledge that he was now the leader of the Comanche tribes. Hurriedly, Nocona questioned the boy about the battle that had just taken place.

The attack had come swiftly, the boy told them. It was short, sharp, and ended soon after it had started. The Tonkawas who were accompanying the group of rangers had led the attack against Pohebits Quasho and his family. Not one Comanche brave had escaped, for no brave would give up the fight. An Indian would accept death before capture. The women and children had been made prisoners. The young boy himself was away from his camp at the time so that he was not seen by the raiders.

Chief Pohebits Quasho had dressed himself in his full battle dress, including his head-dress covered with colored feathers and red flannel strips. He had hurriedly rubbed war paint on his face. Then he had dashed up and down between the opposing lines on his horse, shouting and teasing the white enemies and their Indian companions. After the fight with the Tonkawas, one of them named Jim Pockmark shot Pohebits Quasho. He fell in the dust.

But now, another group under the careful Peta Nocona was marching through the hills north of the Canadian. About one o'clock in the afternoon the rangers had just met after the killing of Pohebits Quasho's fighters. They were just in time to see Nocona ride up to the top of the hill above them with his large group of Indian followers. The new men held their horses at the top of the hill, waiting to see what the enemy would do now.

The wives and older youths had taken their places at a distance from the scene. They could hear the shouting of the angry warriors. Preloch sighed as she saw the flash of sunlight on the rifles of the enemy. She feared for the baby riding behind her. She knew that it would take very much hard work for her people to defeat these white men. The rifle gave him an edge that would be hard to overcome by just a bow and arrow or a lance. She was afraid of this weapon that the white men used.

The order was given for the Tonkawa chief, Old Placido, to move toward the Comanche warriors. This was done in order to draw the Comanches into the valley in the hope that it would give the rangers a better chance to charge them. Nocona ordered his men to charge against the Tonkawas who were wearing white badges on their heads. This fact made them easy targets for Nocona and his braves. It also made things difficult for the rangers. In the fury of the fighting, they could not tell one Indian from another.

The Tonkawas had to be withdrawn so that they could take off their white badges. Nocona with his men watched this move, and then they began to prepare for the next charge from the whites. It was with this next charge that the Comanche line was broken. There followed a running fight that ranged for three or four miles. During all of this time, Preloch and the other women had begun falling back toward their camp. As the Comanches moved back, the women hurried their own movement in order to try to warn those remaining in the camp.

Nocona, as was his practice, succeeded in covering their path by good planning and movement. True to Comanche teaching, he must protect the women and children from harm as long as possible. The Comanches made one final hard stand in a tree-covered gully, where many of Nocona's men were killed.

The ranger leader ordered a halt to the fight about four o'clock, and his men returned to their camp. The battle of Antelope Hills was a victory for the rangers. They had lost only two men with five or six wounded. The Comanches counted their dead and missing as seventy-five. After punishing the Comanches so soundly, the rangers returned to their fort.

Nocona, Preloch, and their children moved with the remaining tribes back toward the western Palo Duro Canyon strongholds. It would take the tribes many long, back-breaking weeks of work to bring back their old way of life. All the buffalo robes, tepees, food, and other belongings had been left on the banks of the Canadian River along the Antelope Hills.

In the following years, there were many other battles with groups of rangers, but none was quite so bad as this fight at Antelope Hills. The Comanche brave would long remember the wild fight which he put up here on the Canadian River. It didn't serve to break the Comanche spirit, but it certainly did much to make him hate the white man.

Nursing her baby girl, Preloch sat in the shade of a giant cottonwood tree in the confines of Palo Duro Canyon. She thought about the former times with her Comanche family. There had been good times when they had succeeded in defeating their enemies. Many were the times when a raiding party had sat all night on a hillside to await the coming dawn so that they could ride into camp in the full glory of morning. They were welcomed home as real heroes with their trophies of the raid, horses, goods, and scalp locks.

Preloch remembered the time when Nocona had led the parade of black-painted fighters into camp. There was the shouting and singing by the entire tribe. All had been joy in the camp that day. Nocona had carried his lance high, covered with the scalps that he had taken in this fight. The others had followed with their own booty on display. With the scalp poles held high so that all could see, the warriors had paraded into the village.

As they came to their own lodges, the returning braves had turned their horses and weapons over to a wife, mother, or sister. Then he had gone inside to rest. Later they would prepare for the Scalp Dance which would come that evening. When the braves returned without scalps, then they called the dance simply a Victory Dance. But dance they did, regardless of the prizes won.

This particular night all the scalps were tied to a scalp pole that had been built in the center of the dance area. They had gathered wood and stacked it for their bonfire. Everyone had dressed for the party. At this time the women wore black paint while the men wore red paint. The dance began with the women lined up opposite the men. Each line danced forward and backward; then the group formed a circle when they danced around the scalp pole. Preloch watched Nocona proudly as she glided through the steps of the familiar dance.

As the dancing continued through the night, it became wilder and wilder. There were no captives on this occasion; so the torture of the captives could not be enjoyed. Preloch was glad for this fact. She had a very faint remembrance of the time when she too was a captive. Time had blotted out most of the memory of that past. She was glad that she did not have to think about those times any more.

A noise above her resting spot awoke Preloch to the present time. She saw her sons returning from the brief trip out above the canyon walls to try their hands at hunting some antelope or deer. Gradually, the tribe was restoring their former life. With the fall hunting season, they would have all of the things that they needed for life throught the winter time. Their tepees were rebuilt, and now slowly they were replacing their worn and ragged clothing. Quanah had promised her a new antelope skin for a dress.

Preloch watched as the boys unloaded the meat and skins that they had brought to their mother. She smiled as she saw the antelope hide that Quanah was unpacking from the back of his horse. She would have that new dress as soon as she could cure and tan the hide. The horror of the Antelope Hills battle was over. They would live a happy life once again.

# 5.  The Recapture of Cynthia Ann

Preloch had no way of knowing that her present way of life was about to end so soon. Even though she feared the white man's rifle, she did not know that weapon would bring an end to her Indian ways.

Nocona and his braves were just riding into camp one afternoon on a beautiful day. Preloch and the other wives ran forward to greet them and to take their horses. This was a great victory that they would honor this night. The braves had just raided in Parker County, the land were Preloch's relatives now lived. Nocona and his men had brought many horses and scalps back to camp.

It was the fall of 1860, and the Comanches had done great damage to the little settlements in Parker County. Captain Sul Ross was gathering his forces to lead them against the hostile Comanches and to punish them for their raids on white settlers. The outcry had become loud among the settlers on the frontiers of Texas.

But fear of this army did not dim the joy of the Comanche celebrations. There would be an exciting scalp dance this night. They knew little of the coming events. In fact, they cared little because today the Comanche had proven his great power. The parties would last all night and into the following night before the happy braves would be worn into sleep.

A few days after they had gotten over the effects of the wild scalp dance, Preloch and a large group of women and some captive slaves prepared to leave for a last hunt before the winter set in. Meanwhile, Nocona and his two sons were out hunting for new winter camp sites. It was now December and soon the icy winds would blow across the Llano Estacado.

Preloch told her husband and her sons goodbye, and then she set out for the Pease River hunting grounds. She had her baby, Prairie Flower, with her. In order to take care of them, Nocona had sent his Mexican slave, whom they called "Nocona's Joe" or simply "Joe Nocona." Joe had been given careful orders to protect Preloch and the baby against any harm that might happen to them.

The hunting party located a huge herd of buffalo just north of the present town of Crowell, Texas, near the Pease River. The men prepared the drying packs while the women set up the tepees for their short stay here. In the early afternoon a wild dust storm hurt their efforts. However, they continued to make the camp livable. They were not very careful to set out the usual guards. The high winds that blew everything about made it very unlikely that they would be bothered. Perhaps they thought that no one would come out during such bad weather conditions. Whatever the cause, this failure to do so allowed the white soldiers to approach the camp and to surprise the tribe.

Perhaps because of the wind or because of their eager desire to drive the Comanches from Texas, Captain Ross's forces attacked the group that was mainly women and children. It was later brought out that they could not tell that the heavily wrapped figures were women instead of men. In fact, until the fight was over, they did not know the true nature of the camp they had attacked.

As soon as the attack began, the Indians started mounting their horses to escape. Preloch and her baby girl were riding one horse. Joe Nocona was mounted on another horse with a young Indian girl riding behind him. Captain Ross chased Joe Nocona. He shot the girl, but Joe escaped injury from that shot because he was wearing his shield on his back. It turned away the shot that killed the girl.

Lieutenant Kelliheir was following the horse that ran out of the camp beside that of Joe Nocona. It carried Preloch and her baby girl. Joe tried to led the soldiers away from Preloch, but he was not successful in his attempt to save her. Lieutenant Kelliheir grabbed the reins of her horse and stopped it not far away from the spot where Captain Ross was shooting at Joe, but it was too late. Captain Ross's shot had hit Joe in the arm. Before Joe could urge his horse on, Captain Ross again shot him twice, the shot going through Joe's body twice and breaking his right arm.

Joe fell from his horse. He rose in spite of the pain and walked to a nearby tree. Joe leaned up against the tree and began to sing. Preloch knew the death song that he was singing. She knew that Joe could not help her any more. He was dying.

Preloch's robe fell from her face, and Lieutenant Kelliheir screamed out to Captain Ross.

"Hey, this ain't no Indian. It's a white woman with blonde hair and blue eyes. She's got a baby with her!"

Preloch didn't understand their words. She feared for her life. She tried to make them understand with the two words of English that she still remembered. "Me 'merican! Me 'merican!"

The men helped her down from her horse. She held Prairie Flower tightly in her arms. She still didn't understand that they were not going to shoot her. Preloch cried and sobbed as the men discussed what to do with her. Her Indian companions had been slain or had fled in panic. There was no one here to help her now. Finally, Captain Ross decided that she was just afraid, not mourning for her dead companion. He called his Mexican helper to try to talk to her.

The man told Preloch that she must not be afraid of the white men. He said that they knew she was a white woman. They would take her back to her white people where she would be cared for.

Preloch told him that she was afraid for her two boys, who had remained with her husband, Peta Nocona. She was worried about what would become of Pecos and Quanah. If they should come to look for her, the white men might kill them. At this thought, Preloch began to sob loudly. The night seemed to her as though it would never end. Her sadness overcame her, but finally she slept.

When morning finally came, the men set off with their poor, frightened captives, Preloch and her baby Prairie Flower, for Camp Cooper, which was near present day Albany, Texas. Captain N. G. Evans was in command of the Unites States Cavalry station-ed at Camp Cooper. Mrs. Evans, the wife of Captain Evans, took charge of Preloch. Along with the other officers' wives, she did her best to make the captives comfortable. They bathed Prairie Flower and dressed her in baby clothes that one wife brought to Preloch. They also gave Preloch new clothing to replace the ragged antelope dress she had arrived in.

Preloch, in spite of the kind treatment, was very sad and unhappy in this new dress. She missed her soft antelope hide dress. These clothes were stiff and binding on her body. They offered her food, but she sometimes refused to eat because it did not taste right to her. She would have liked some of her carefully

made pemmican to chew on. She slept on the floor
with her baby. She could not get used to the soft bed
which they gave her. This life made her very
unhappy. She longed for the carefree days on the
Llano Estacado, wearing buffalo robes and eating
fresh buffalo meat.

Colonel Ross sent some men to tell her uncle
Issac Parker in Weatherford, Texas, of her capture.
Issac left immediately for Camp Cooper. Colonel Ross
had left word for his Mexican servant to go with Issac
from Fort Belknap to Camp Cooper. The ladies tried
to tell Preloch about her uncle, but she could not
understand what they were trying to say to her. She

just nodded when they asked her if she understood. Actually, she did not know what they meant.

Preloch at this time was thirty-four years old. It had been twenty-four years since she had seen her uncle. The name Issac did not mean anything to her. Strange as it may seem, no one bothered to call her by her name of "Cynthia Ann." The name she gave them was "Preloch," and that is what they called her.

Colonel Parker arrived, and he was convinced almost at once that she was the long lost Cynthia Ann. He tried to talk with her through the Mexican interpreter. She remembered nothing of the things that he tried to tell her. She could not remember anything about her family. Almost in despair, Colonel Parker told her that his niece's name was "Cynthia Ann." The old familiar name brought a response from the sad unhappy Preloch. She looked up at him and patted her breast and said, "Cynthia Ann! Cynthia Ann!" Colonel Parker was very happy at these words from his niece.

Within the week Cynthia Ann and Prairie Flower left Camp Cooper in the company of her uncle Issac and the men he had brought with him from Weatherford. They took her to Issac Parker's home in Birdville, a town just outside of Fort Worth, Texas. It was a long, hard trip for Cynthia Ann, who had known no other way of travel than the Indian pony which she had ridden most of her life. The wagon was very uncomfortable and rough to her. The sounds of the strange voices made her afraid.

She understood that Issac was her uncle, but he was still a stranger to her. Several times she tried to escape when they camped at night. Guards had to be set up to keep her from running away. Issac talked to her almost constantly, trying to reach her, to make her remember the white family that had once been hers. He was patient with her, but it was very hard for Cynthia Ann.

Issac was afraid that he would never be able to talk to Cynthia Ann in English. The day that she called him "Uncle Issac" would be a time that he would remember the rest of his life. From that time on, she seemed to get along better in this new way of life. She became interested in the spinning that the women showed her. Soon she was working at the spinning wheel for hours at a time. It kept her mind busy so that she could forget for a while about her sons.

The only thing that remained truly different for her was sleeping. She could not rest in the bed that they gave her. So she was allowed to make a pallet on the floor where she and Prairie Flower could sleep. That was the only thing which she could not accept. The rest of her nights were spent on a pallet.

One of the most fearful times in this new life for Cynthia Ann was the time when she was taken to Austin. The Secession Convention was meeting. She sat in the meeting room, looking at the strange faces. They looked back at her in interested stares. She remembered the tales that she had heard from her Comanche people about the Council House meeting in San Antonio. She hugged Prairie Flower tighter and kept her eyes trained on the floor. She couldn't bear to look at these men. They might even kill her baby, too, as they had done in San Antonio.

"Cynthia Ann, don't be so frightened," one of the ladies said to her. "They aren't going to hurt you. They are just talking about whether or not Texas is going to secede from the Union."

Cynthia Ann did not understand the word

"secede." It meant nothing to her. She knew that Texas was where her people lived but the Union was too much for her to think about. If only she could go back to her Comanche people! They would not worry about such things.

What did worry Cynthia Ann was the past. She feared for the lives of her sons, Quanah and Pecos. Sometimes some word came to the settlement about the raids that the boys had carried out. Cynthia Ann's feeling were torn at the thought that her sons might be killed in one of these raids. She knew that she should be sad about the bad things they said her sons had done. However, she knew that they might be killed. Her fear for their safety was greater than her sorrow.

"I want my sons," she told her relatives. "I am afraid that they will be killed." She rarely talked about her husband, Nocona. Her thoughts were for the most part about her sons and the care of her little daughter, Prairie Flower. Her children were always the center of her life. She lived in the hope that some day she could be with her sons again.

Sometimes, reports came in about Nocona and his sons. They had moved far out in the Plains where they still carried out savage raids on the settlers who were slowly moving to the Comanche range land.

One day her uncle Issac came to see her and put his arm around her shoulders. He wasn't sure how she would take the news that he had come to give her. He knew that she had not mentioned Nocona to him very often, but surely she would cry about the story he had just heard.

"Cynthia Ann, I am sorry," he said. "I must tell you what I heard in town today. One of the rangers came in yesterday with a story about the great chief,

Nocona. He had heard the story from a trapper who had just come in from the mountains in northern New Mexico." Issac paused as he looked into Cynthia Ann's eyes. "Nocona is dead from a bad wound."

She made no movement and made no sound. No tears came to her eyes. Softly, she said to Issac, "Chief, he whip too much."

That was the last word that Cynthia Ann said about her husband. His memory was in the past, and she seemed to forget about him. However, now her worry about her sons became even greater. She talked of them all the time, wishing they could be with her. She no longer talked of going back to "her People." That was now the past for her. She knew that it was over. She ceased to think of the past.

But more sad news was to come for Cynthia Ann. It was only a short time later that she was told of the death of her son, Pecos. This news too had come through traders who had gone into Comanche territory. After this last blow, Cynthia Ann just seemed to fade away. She did become very active in spinning and weaving for the Confederate War cause. This was an activity that held her interest and kept her from thinking so much about her past life.

Cynthia Ann spent many hours working at the loom and playing with little Prairie Flower, who was learning to talk. Cynthia Ann tried to teach her about the life of her father's people. She feared that Prairie Flower would grow up with the white people and forget her way of Indian life. She had been so young when she had been torn from her family. The young forget so very easily.

The final blow for Cynthia Ann came in 1864 when the doctor had to be called in the middle of the night to tend to young Prairie Flower. They told her that Prairie Flower had been taken ill with spinal meningitis, a white man's disease. The young body had not been able to overcome the effects of the disease. Two days later the baby was gone. Cynthia Ann was broken hearted. Life was over for her. All of her interest in life was gone.

Her relatives decided that she should go to the home of her brother-in-law to recover from the death of her baby. But it was all useless. Cynthia Ann pined her life away in mourning for her two lost children. Shortly after she arrived at the home in Anderson County, Cynthia Ann died. Her troubles were finally over.

Prairie Flower's tiny body was brought to Anderson County to be buried with that of Cynthia Ann. But could Cynthia Ann have known that this was not to be her final resting place, she would probably have been happy. Her son, Quanah, had not forgotten his mother. Long after her death, the son now living on a reservation in Oklahoma, began to search for his mother's grave. Just as she had not been able to forget him, he too had been unable to forget the mother who had meant so very much to him.

Quanah advertised in Texas newspapers for a picture of his beloved mother. Colonel Sul Ross, who had been on the Pease River where Cynthia Ann had been recaptured, saw Quanah's advertisement. He knew that a picture had been made by a photographer in Fort Worth, Texas. The picture showed Cynthia Ann nursing Prairie Flower. S. B. Burnett, a wealthy Texas cattleman, had become good friends with Quanah, from whom he had leased land in Oklahoma. Burnett had the picture copied in oils and sent to Quanah.

After the success with the picture, Quanah

began to work toward having his mother's remains moved to the reservation in Oklahoma. The husband of one of Quanah's daughters was given permission to locate and to identify Cynthia Ann's remains and to have them brought to Cache, Oklahoma, for burial. He found her grave located in Fosterville cemetery. The remains were placed in a new casket with Prairie Flower's remains placed as though she were in her mother's arms.

The son-in-law was with Quanah when he viewed the remains. Quanah asked if he was certain that it was Cynthia Ann. When assured that it was, he said then, "I am satisfied. I have looked for a long time."

Cynthia Ann Parker was reburied on December 10, 1910. Quanah followed her in death within two months, February 21, 1911. He was laid to rest at her side. At long last the mother and her son were reunited in death as they could not be in life. Later the remains of all three, Cynthia Ann Parker, Prairie Flower, and Quanah Parker, were removed to Fort Sill, Oklahoma. At this time the man who gave the funeral oration said that Cynthia Ann Parker was a shining example of troubled motherhood everywhere.

10.77

ATE DUE

# 198                              10.77

| DATE DUE | BORROWER'S NAME | ROOM NUMBER |
|---|---|---|
|  |  |  |
|  |  |  |
|  |  |  |
|  |  |  |